LOSELEY PARK

Historic Home of the More-Molyneux Family

My family and I welcome you to Loseley Park. The House was built by an ancestor to entertain Queen Elizabeth I and since then each generation has made its own contribution.

Loseley is also an agricultural estate and a business. There has never been great wealth in the family and most generations have been involved in public service as well as in managing the property. My grandfather started the Jersey herd and home farm and, together with my grandmother, held on during the difficult war years, living in the House without electricity, heating or hot water to save it from decay. My father and mother, after the war, developed the farming business and founded Guildway Limited, which started with the production of concrete blocks and progressed to the construction of pre-fabricated houses which were exported all over the world. Profit sharing and joint consultation, which were started in 1951, together with the opening of Loseley House and the founding of Loseley Dairy Products in 1968, have all played a major part in Loseley's recovery.

Whether you have come to Loseley for a visit to the House and Gardens, or for a corporate activity, wedding reception, conference or any other function, we all hope very much that you will enjoy your time here.

In these pages we bring to your notice the main works of interest to be seen at Loseley. The house is still the home of the family who built it in the reign of Elizabeth I, and we feel that it is in the interests of all that the friendly lived-in atmosphere of our home should be preserved. We welcome you as visitors. Barriers and labels are reduced to a minimum and it will greatly assist in the preservation of works of art and books if you will kindly refrain from touching them. Much that you will see at Loseley dates back to the Elizabethan period when the house was built. Some pieces are older than the house itself and each succeeding generation has added its contribution of furniture, books and paintings, down to the photographs of the present generations. If you wish for information which is not given here, your guide will try to help, but the answer may have passed into antiquity.

Over the inner door of the Entrance Hall you will see a Latin inscription: Invidiae claudor, pateo sed semper amico. This may be loosely translated as 'I am shut to envy, but always open to a friend'. We welcome you as a friend and hope you will enjoy your visit.

Michael More-Molyneux

THE BUILDING

Sir Christopher More, a direct ancestor of the present owner, and Sheriff of Surrey and Sussex, bought the Manor of Loseley, with the old house which stood near the site of the present mansion, in the reign of King Henry VII.

Sir William More, son of Sir Christopher, built the present house in the reign of Queen Elizabeth during the years 1562-1568. Sir William, one of the Queen's most trusted advisers, supervised the building work himself, and his original accounts of the building are preserved. The total cost of the house was £1,640 19s. 7d.

Most of the building stone, now over 860 years old, came from the ruins of the Cistercian Waverley Abbey, near Farnham, which was pulled down by Henry VIII. The stone contributes greatly to the mellow appearance and atmosphere of the house. The clunch facings came from a quarry in Guildford and pillars were built of stone from the quarries at Hascombe Hill.

As can be seen in the old paintings of Loseley (and on the front cover), there was a further wing to the North West, containing a chapel, picture gallery 121 feet long, and a riding school. Built by Sir George More at the beginning of the 17th century, this wing fell into disrepair and was pulled down in 1820. To the North East stands the original garden wall, in which can be seen the archways which matched those in the wing opposite. Part of the original moat is still in existence and was connected by a secret passage, now sealed off, to the cellars.

Photo: Nicola Stocken Tomkins

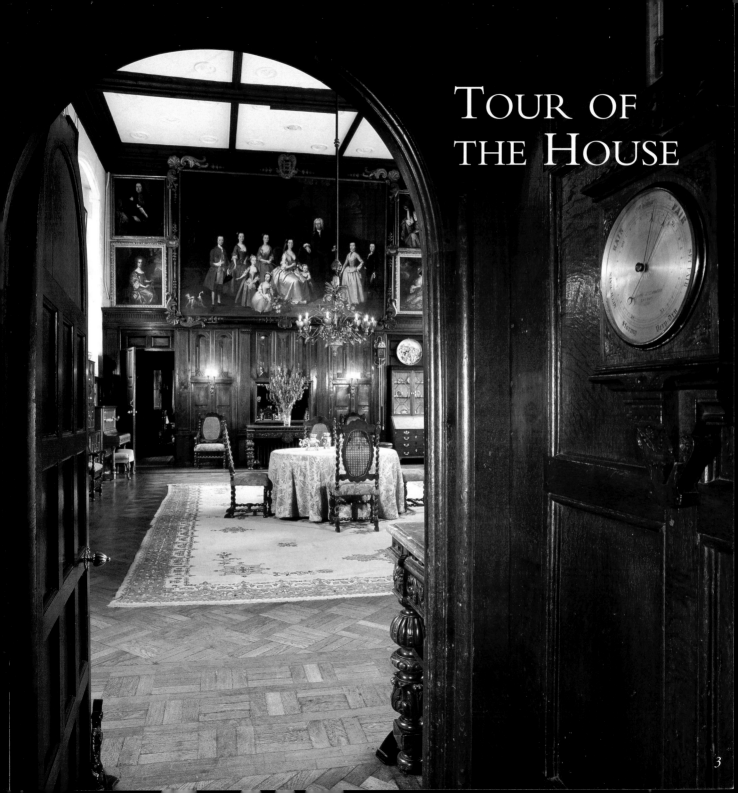

TOUR OF THE HOUSE

In the Entrance Hall stands a marble table on an alabaster support, featuring the Tudor Rose and Scottish Thistle. This was made for King Henry VIII and came from Nonsuch Palace. On entering the Great Hall in the right hand corner hangs a portrait of Mary Queen of Scots. Full-length portraits of King James I and his Queen (left), hang on the South wall. These were painted by the court painter John de Critz and presented by the King to Loseley in commemoration of his visits. The large jewel in James I's hat is the 'Mirror of Great Britain' which was made in 1604, soon after the union of the Scottish and English Crowns. Above James I is a small portrait of King Charles II.

King Edward VI

On the far wall is a very large picture of Sir More Molyneux with his wife, Cassandra, and eight of their eleven children. This was painted by Somers, in the Hall, in 1739.

To the left of the fireplace hangs a very fine portrait of the boy King Edward VI. He is wearing the Great Collar of Henry VIII which also appears in the Chatsworth cartoon of Henry VIII in the National Portrait Gallery. Above Edward VI is a 1937 portrait of Brigadier General Francis More-Molyneux-Longbourne CMG, DSO, father of James More-Molyneux. Above the General is a portrait of James More-Molyneux OBE DL and on his right a portrait of his wife Susan. Top right of the fireplace is Admiral Sir Robert More-Molyneux.

Brigadier General Francis More-Molyneux-Longbourne CMG, DSO

With the exception of the photograph of HM Queen Mary, taken on her visit in 1932, and Their Royal Highnesses the Earl and Countess of Wessex taken on their visit in 2002, all other portraits in the Hall not mentioned above are of members of the family.

Admiral Sir Robert More-Molyneux

The Hall panelling came from Henry VIII's Nonsuch Palace when it was demolished. Nonsuch was built for Katherine Parr, and one of the panels bears her initials, while others have 'H R' and the portcullis of Henry VIII.

The Dutch carved wood and gilt bracket clock beneath the large picture bears the date 1537.

The painted glass coats of arms in the Hall windows are original and are mentioned in the builder's accounts as 'Ij armes in my haule wyndowe'. On one pane of glass in the South Alcove is depicted a scene in a mill, showing the grinding stones, the wheat being fed into the hoppers and the miller loading a wagon with flour. The date is 1662. Above the Gallery hang panels which were painted by the Italian, Toto del Nunziata, for King Henry VIII's banqueting tents. These depict classical gods and mythical characters. The guidon is that of the Surrey Volunteer Cavalry, of the Napoleonic era.

In the South Alcove is George IV's coronation chair: this is the chair in which the sovereign is anointed as spiritual head. This chair is given to the Dean, the chair in which the sovereign is crowned remains in Westminster Abbey.

The carving on the Minstrels' Gallery is by Grinling Gibbons.

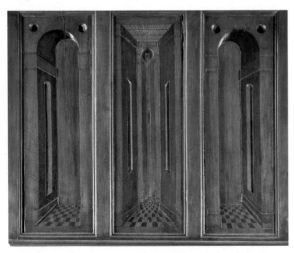

Even more striking is the trompe l'oeil of the wooden panels at the far end of the Hall. The carving, not more than a quarter of an inch deep, gives the impression of long corridors.

THE LIBRARY

Leaving the Great Hall by the West door, the first room on the right is the Library. Sir William More was one of the first English gentlemen to create a library. Besides the fine collection of books, built up by successive generations of the family, should be mentioned a carved piece of wood above the mantelpiece (above).

This bears the arms and initials of Queen Elizabeth I to commemorate her visits to Loseley, and is dated 1570. The inscription above the bookshelves (right), Aversos compono animos et saecula cogo means, referring to a book, 'I soothe troubled minds and while away the centuries'. There is a fine picture of Venice painted by Russell, a member of the English School.

Above the door is a painting of Loseley, showing the old wing before it was pulled down in 1820 having fallen into disrepair. The wing contained a chapel, riding school and picture gallery.

Photo: George R. Titus

THE DRAWING ROOM

At the end of the passage is the Drawing Room.
This room is beautifully proportioned with a gilded ceiling decorated for James I's visit. The moorhens, cockatrices and mulberry trees which adorn the frieze are family emblems. The motto Morus tarde moriens morum cito moriturum around the mulberry tree is, of course, a pun on the family name of More and means 'The mulberry tree dying slowly, the fruit about to die quickly'. The family, like the tree, will survive for a long time, but the individual Mores, like the fruit, enjoy a relatively brief existence. The tree fell down during the 1939-45 war, but to the great relief of the family did not die - as you can see in the walled garden. The chimneypiece in this room is unique, being carved out of a solid block of chalk. Such intricate work, to a Holbein design, would have demanded great skill from a wood carver, but in chalk it is a fantastic achievement. By the hearth are two Elizabethan Maid of Honour chairs, the cushions of which are believed to have been worked by Queen Elizabeth. They have been exhibited at several Tudor exhibitions and are in excellent condition. On the left of the chimneypiece hangs a portrait of the builder of the house, Sir William More. The skull in the picture is a reminder that death will come and that the mind should not get too absorbed with earthly matters. This portrait is also of particular interest as it is the only known portrait by the Flemish artist Lucas de Heere.

Mrs. Lowndes-Stone, a copy from the original by Gainsborough

The portrait above Sir William More is of Sir Thomas More, the Chancellor, who is a connection of the family by marriage. Sir Christopher More's sister Alice married the widower Judge Sir John More and thus became the Chancellor's stepmother.

Sir George More, Sir William's son, has his portrait by Jansen on the North side of the East Wall, and next to him, in armour, is Sir Poynings More, Bt., his grandson. In the centre of the East Wall is a strikingly lovely portrait of Mrs. Lowndes-Stone, an ancestor. This is a copy of the original by Gainsborough, now in the Gulbenkian Collection.

Next is a fine portrait by Jansen of the bearded Robert More, son of Sir George and father of Sir Poynings. The delicate and finely clothed youth near the doorway is a Mr. Rous, probably Christopher Rous of Henham, Suffolk, who was the first husband of Poynings More's wife Elizabeth, also believed to be by Jansen. The oval portrait on the other side of the doorway is of Anne Boleyn (left). Next, in armour again, is another good portrait of the adventurous Sir Poynings More, by Dobson.

The flower painting on glass, inscribed Rosa Electa was done for Queen Elizabeth, 'the Elect Rose'. Many of the Queen's symbolic flowers are gathered into this basket.

The dramatic sea picture (right), depicting the wreck of the two ships in a storm, is by Willem Van der Velde who specialised in sea paintings and was court painter to King Charles II. The date of this picture is 1696. On the right, the dark lady in blue is the Duchess of

Chandos, a close friend of the family at the time of the painting of the group in the Great Hall (1739). Near the North window is a fine English Queen Anne cabinet with seaweed design depicting St. Francis fishing. The large arm-chairs and the fine walnut settee are Georgian. On the left of the door is an excellent example of English lacquer cabinet work.

Perhaps the most remarkable piece of furniture in the house is the cabinet near the fireplace. This is a sixteenth century South German Wrangelschrank, of which there are few surviving examples. It is of pinewood, inlaid with pearwood, rosewood, beech, sycamore, Hungarian ash and other woods. The design is of a fallen city, with broken pillars covered in vegetation and every detail is perfect.

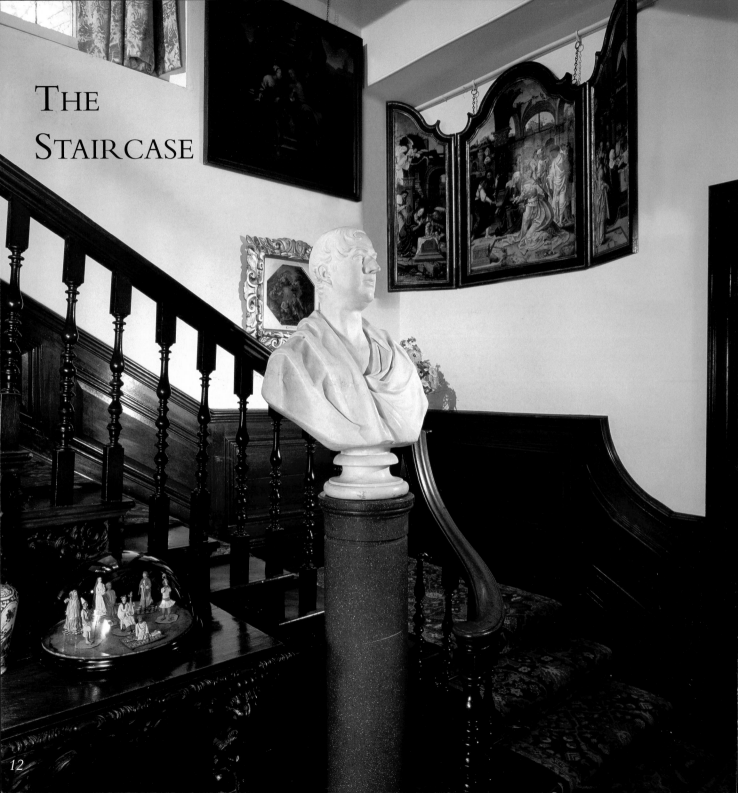

The
Staircase

The pictures hanging on the walls on the main staircase to the bedrooms depict the life and death of Our Lord. The upper staircase is mainly devoted to the manifestation of God's power after the Resurrection and Ascension. Further pictures are in the Thomas More Room. For further details of the Loseley Christian Trust, please visit the Chapel or Thomas More Room.

Detail of the Triptych:
The Nativity by
The Master of Antwerp.
Adoration of the Shepherds, The Magi,
The Presentation in the Temple.
Early 16th Century, Flemish

THE BEDROOMS

*The first bedroom on the right is Sir More's Room. The furnishing includes
a large fourposter bed and a fine 18th century Vauxhall mirror. The oak
court cupboard bears the date 1697.*

Nautilus Cup depicting the Seven Labours of Hercules, King's Room Cabinet, presented to Admiral Sir Robert More-Molyneux

Photo: George R. Titus

At the end of another short passage on the right is the room occupied by King James I, and known as the King's Room (above). The carpet features the Tudor Rose, Crown and Thistle in the King's honour. The tapestries are Oudenarde, of about 1650.

Queen Elizabeth's Room adjoins the King's Room, and the tapestry is Mortlake, of the Charles II period. A clue to the story is given by the name 'David' on the man's garter and it is the meeting of David and Abigail. The other tapestry is

Antwerp and shows King Saul. The delicate carving over the fireplace depicts the story of the Good Samaritan and is thought to be 17th century German.

The hand-made bed and window curtains and the carved oak pelmet, showing a boar hunt taking place, are worth noting. These are original. The bedcover is of the William and Mary period. It was greatly admired by H.M. Queen Mary on her visit in 1932 – so much so that she arranged for it to be shown in various needlework exhibitions.

THE MORES
OF LOSELEY

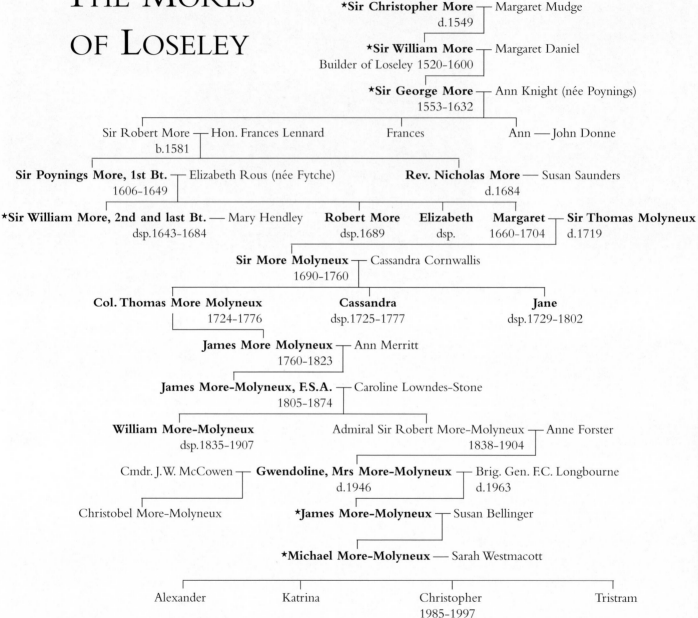

★Sir Christopher More ─ Margaret Mudge
d.1549

★Sir William More ─ Margaret Daniel
Builder of Loseley 1520–1600

★Sir George More ─ Ann Knight (née Poynings)
1553–1632

Sir Robert More ─ Hon. Frances Lennard   Frances   Ann ── John Donne
b.1581

Sir Poynings More, 1st Bt. ─ Elizabeth Rous (née Fytche)   **Rev. Nicholas More** ── Susan Saunders
1606–1649   d.1684

★Sir William More, 2nd and last Bt. ── Mary Hendley   **Robert More**   **Elizabeth**   **Margaret** ─ **Sir Thomas Molyneux**
dsp.1643–1684   dsp.1689   dsp.   1660–1704   d.1719

Sir More Molyneux ─ Cassandra Cornwallis
1690–1760

Col. Thomas More Molyneux   **Cassandra**   **Jane**
1724–1776   dsp.1725–1777   dsp.1729–1802

James More Molyneux ─ Ann Merritt
1760–1823

James More-Molyneux, F.S.A. ─ Caroline Lowndes-Stone
1805–1874

William More-Molyneux   Admiral Sir Robert More-Molyneux ─ Anne Forster
dsp.1835–1907   1838–1904

Cmdr. J.W. McCowen ─ **Gwendoline, Mrs More-Molyneux** ─ Brig. Gen. F.C. Longbourne
d.1946   d.1963

Christobel More-Molyneux   **★James More-Molyneux** ─ Susan Bellinger

★Michael More-Molyneux ── Sarah Westmacott

Alexander   Katrina   Christopher   Tristram
1985–1997

Bold type denotes owners of the estate

★ High Sheriff of Surrey

Sir Christopher More was an Exchequer official in Henry VII's reign who rose to be King's Remembrancer under Henry VIII. A Londoner of Derbyshire extraction, he bought Loseley Manor in 1508 and lived in the medieval house situated on what is now the South Lawn. He took an active part in the affairs of the country and was twice Sheriff of Surrey and Sussex.

Sir Christopher's son, Sir William More, held many high offices and was a personal friend and trusted adviser of Queen Elizabeth. Sir William inherited Loseley in 1549 and commenced building the present house in 1562. Queen Elizabeth I stayed at Loseley on four occasions. A letter to Sir William More, still preserved, gives strict instructions concerning the preparations for one of the Queen's visits. Straw was to be strewn on the drive to avoid jolting of the carriage, Sir William to 'Avoyde his family' i.e. evacuate his family and servants to make room for the Queen's retinue, and the house must be cleaner than on the last occasion!

Sir William More

Lady More, wife of Sir William More

It appears that Sir William planned the house himself and was also 'Clerk of the Works', supervising the work of his own direct labour. For a man with many public duties to perform, this was no mean task. Queen Elizabeth knighted Sir William in 1576, with the comment that he 'well deserved the honour'.

The Earl of Southampton, a 'suspected Papist', was for some time in the custody of Sir William at Loseley where he was treated with consideration and courtesy.

Sir George More, by Jansen

Sir George More inherited Loseley on the death of his father, Sir William, in 1600. He represented both Guildford and Surrey in Parliament, and was created Chancellor of the Order of the Garter by King James I who twice stayed at Loseley. Sir George was also Lieutenant of the Tower of London and Treasurer to Henry Prince of Wales. He consolidated the family's position by buying the Manor and Hundred of Godalming from the Crown in 1601 for £1,341 8s. 23/4d.

A son-in-law of Sir George wrote an obituary of his father-in-law, whom he held in very high esteem: 'He was but little of stature, but of great abilities. By nature very passionate, yet in his wisdom he conquered that passion so much that you would think him to be of a mild disposition. His only error among his many admirable virtues was that he much neglected his own affairs. It was his misery to live in an age wherein good and understanding men's merits were valued at less than ill and weak men's money. He was ever more ready and willing to do courtesies for others than for himself . . . the most temperate and the greatest painstaker that ever I knew, and an honester man never lived. He was the ablest, most understanding gentleman that ever I knew and, withal, the most active in business. There was no place or employment but he was fit for it ... He was little and good'. There is an interesting note on Sir George's housekeeping at Loseley: 'He kept 50 liveries, spent every week an ox and 12 sheep . . .'

One of Sir George More's daughters, Ann, was secretly married at 17 years old, to John Donne, later Dr. Donne, the well-known poet and Dean of St. Paul's - 'never send to know for whom the bell tolls; it tolls for thee'. Sir George was furious when he discovered the marriage and had Donne deprived of office and imprisoned in the notorious Fleet Prison for a year. Donne wrote 'John Donne, Ann Donne, undone'. Reconciliation followed and the marriage was very happy. In 1617 Ann died at the age of 33 after giving birth to their twelfth child. John was heartbroken and never remarried. Ann's memorial tablet in St. Clement Danes Church, London, destroyed in the blitz has been renewed and was dedicated in the crypt in 1986. On the death of Sir George More in 1632, his grandson, Poynings More, succeeded to Loseley. Poynings was an adventurous and gallant gentleman. Among the Loseley

MSS is preserved a 'licence and passeport' for three years, from Lords of the Council to Poynings More of Loseley, co. Surrey, who 'is desirous to travell into Forraine partes and therein to remaine for the space of three yeares of the date hereof, for the gaining of Language and bettering his experience'. Most young men who go abroad to-day do so on the same pretext as did Poynings over 300 years ago! Both the portraits of Poynings More show him in armour, and he was undoubtedly a man of action. He was created a baronet in 1642, shortly before his death, the title becoming extinct on the death of his son and successor, Sir William More, without issue, in 1684. From the Rev. Nicholas More, younger brother of Poynings, Loseley passed to Robert More, who died unmarried in 1689, when the property was carried by his sister Margaret to her husband, Sir Thomas Molyneux, of the family from whom the Earls of Sefton and Viscounts Molyneux derived.

Thenceforward the family name became More Molyneux. The large family painting in the Great Hall, is of Sir More Molyneux, son of Sir Thomas Molyneux, with his wife, Cassandra, and eight of their eleven children, most of whom were fated to die childless and comparatively young. James, the eldest son, died before his father. Thomas (on the right of the picture) became a colonel in the Foot Guards. The equipment which he bought in 1747 when setting out for service in Flanders as a young ensign included '23 yards of printed cotton' to make hangings for a field bedstead! After his death, unmarried, in 1776 and the deaths in rapid succession of her two elder sisters, Jane (fourth from the left in the picture) became mistress of Loseley. An extremely capable woman, she ruled there for more than 20 years, supervising every detail of household and estate management. She left a mass of meticulous accounts and instructions for housekeeping; her careful management succeeded in putting the estate on its feet again after the extravagances of her brother Thomas. When she died unmarried in 1802, the property went to James More

Molyneux, her nephew, who died in 1823. He was succeeded by his son James, who became a J.P. and D.L. and was very active in public service. William More-Molyneux, J.P., younger son of James, inherited Loseley in 1874 and in 1877 added the Nursery Wing on the South side of the house. William died unmarried in 1907 and was succeeded by Gwendoline, the daughter of his younger brother, Admiral Sir Robert More-Molyneux .

Gwendoline married Brigadier General Francis C. Longbourne (who assumed by Deed Poll the additional names of More-Molyneux), and their son James More-Molyneux became the owner on her death in 1946. General More-Molyneux-Longbourne died in 1963. My father and mother married in 1948. I married Sarah Westmacott in 1980 and we have four children, Alexander, Katrina, Christopher (1985-97) and Tristram. In 1998 my father passed to me the responsibility of maintaining and looking after Loseley for the future generations.

The More-Molyneux Family

Tenants' Rent Audit Supper in the Great Hall, early 19th century. This watercolour can be seen in the passageway outside the Library

LOSELEY TODAY

Many visitors want to know a bit more about life at Loseley. In 1946 my father inherited the property with no money and with death duties to be paid, no heating or electricity and a leaking roof! He and my mother accepted the challenge: Loseley had been in the family for 400 years and was worth working for. There are now three generations living at Loseley: my parents, Sarah and myself, and our children, Alexander, Katrina, Christopher (1985-97) and Tristram.

The estate is 1,400 acres, of which 140 is woodland in hand. We have 200 Jersey cows and young stock, and 650 acres of arable crop - both of these farmed under Farm Business Tenancies.

The Loseley Jersey Herd was founded in 1916 and is now one of the largest in the UK. Up until the early 1990s we had two dairy herds and all the milk went into producing the famous Loseley Dairy Products, a company started by my father in 1968. We commenced with the production of cheese, followed by yoghourt and then ice cream. At peak we were supplying some 1,500 customers in London and the Home Counties, exporting to the Far East, Middle East and also Italy, and our customers included Harrods, Fortnum & Mason's, British Airways and the Royal Opera House to name but a few. In 1985, owing to increased overseas competition, margins being cut and lack of land on which to expand, we decided to sell to Booker PLC and as a consequence have not produced Dairy Products on site for over 10 years. The yoghourt and ice cream production buildings are now rented out to a variety of different businesses, including the charity CHASE.

We also have a Loseley Bakery, owned and managed by Mr Steve Cheeseman, producing quiches and cakes, which are also available from the Loseley Shop, Tea Room, Restaurant and other outlets in the South East.

We have run a profit sharing and joint consultation since 1951.